TANGO, TANGOING:

POEMS & ART

TANGO,

TANGOING:

POEMS & ART

MỘNG-LAN

Second paperback edition

ISBN: 978-0-6151-8800-3

Cover, book design, all artwork and photo by Mong-Lan
www.monglan.com

Published by
Valiant Press
P.O. Box 2771
Sugar Land, Texas 77487

For Lovers

& for J.A.

CONTENTS

ACKNOWLEDGEMENTS

Grateful acknowledgements to the editors and journals in which these poems or a portion thereof were first published:

The Colorado Review, from "Milonga—A Seismology"

Coconut Five, from "Argentine Tango: Observations While Dancing"

New American Writing, from "Milonga—A Seismology"

North American Review, "Tangoing"

Pleiades, from "Argentine Tango" and "Milonga—A Seismology"

Softblow Poetry Journal, from "Argentine Tango: Observations While Dancing"

SOLO Magazine, from "Milonga—A Seismology"

Volt, from "Argentine Tango"

Loving thanks to J.A. for your support and for our many visits to and explorations of Buenos Aires. Deep thanks to my mother, B.T.N., for everything over these years. Appreciative thanks to all of my teachers, in poetry, visual arts and dance. Special thanks to G.P. Guerini for sending me the book on tango lyrics at just the right time.

Grateful thanks to the Stegner Fellowship Program at Stanford University for having given me time to write a portion of this book. Thanks also to the Creative Writing Department at the University of Arizona, Tucson, where this book began to take form. Thanks as well to Paul Hoover, Kevin Prufer, Dara Wier, Cyril Wong, Kirk Patterson, and Osvaldo Lodovico for your encouragement and assistance.

Finally, thanks to the milongas and tango dancers of San Francisco, Dallas, Tucson, New York City, Tokyo, Seoul, Singapore, Bangkok, Heidelberg, Amsterdam, Paris, and of course, our beloved Buenos Aires.

TANGOING

Barrio de tango, luna y misterio,
calles lejanas, ¡cómo estarán!

"Barrio de Tango,"
Homero Manzi, 1942

TANGOING

In Buenos Aires the *tangueros* are tangoing to the *bandoneón's* beat
                                    violin's abandon
                seductive net of music

                            Dancing with a restrained wildness cunning controlled
                                    hearts full

elegantly these men & women   elegantly these bellies proudly protruding
                        beef-eating   dancing to the sensual tango

                        Most are genteel & do not steal other's partners do not stow
                                    knives in their blood

                                        Gliding to the *bandoneón's* breath

                pivoting swift turns slow smooth bitter wild excited
                        blind turns

Spinning night to dawn   their love-lives gouged on their faces   desperate
                    lines deeply
            milongueros expose the history of Argentina
                                        on their visages

Dancing rhythms that bodies unravel an unending night unparalleled
                    oblivion & desire

                                desire to forget the lives

            of misery   To forget Menem
            the military dictatorship   disappearances
                                        life-savings & bonds lost

3

In the *Río de la Plata* tango was born over 100 yrs ago
& carries on
The tango of the lower classes tango of the chic   often
happens at night   in *la alta madrugada*   From Africa came its
syncopated rhythms—

~

The night continues
endlessly
I begin
life over
the questions of my life
come to me in dreams
The questions
come & go The dances
went
& came   The men
came & went

The destitute suddenly poorer
come & go at night
They sift through
trash take paper cardboard & recyclables
away leaving disposable trash
pilfered like feathers
receiving a few pesos
for a few kilos

Courteous some say *Buenas Noches*
with soft eyes   Women & children
barrel away
paper   Men cart
away paper   Trash picked at
vultures at dead bodies

Cab drivers do not have change for a 20 peso bill   A lack of *efectivo*

Anapestic   by magic   the city   the nation & its citizens keep on

                                                    Where is the fire?

                        At night fire burns
                in trash bins on city streets   a huge pyre
                waiting for its sacrifice

                                ~

Out until 5 or 6 in the morning   *milongueros*
embrace sucking each other's blood   They lean
towards each other's hearts   plucking
          Perhaps they will follow each other
home   devour the other

Drinking each other's glances & stares   deriving pleasure in dancing   embracing kicking
          between each other's legs   on crowded floors

                            Eyes scan: whom to dance with   whom to avoid?

Tables & tables of hungry women   predatory men   courteous   disdainful

        Around & around   people draw *ochos*   flick *voleos*   flicks of knives

Walls crumbling

I begin life over I start
to read
skies leaves dawn
The questions of my life
float to me in tangos
The questions come
& go the dreams
the men & women

[Buenos Aires, 2001-2004]

ARGENTINE TANGO: OBSERVATIONS WHILE DANCING

Vení, acercate, no tengas miedo,

. . . .

yo solo quiero contarte un cuento

"Dicen Que Dicen"
Alberto J. Ballesteros, 1930

ARGENTINE TANGO: OBSERVATIONS WHILE DANCING

1

the sensual tango with dancers embracing leaning into
the other like so, forehead to forehead—you will be
bewildered to know that the embrace of the tango is
physical . . . . yet spiritual. because you are communing
with another human being on a physical level, sometimes
you don't know your partner's name.   it doesn't matter
& perhaps it is better if you don't know your partner's
name, political affiliation, likes and dislikes. sometimes
he or she will ask your name at the end of a dance if
there is affinity. but one's name is not the issue. what is
important is the conversation through gestures, pressures,
and geometric shapes made through and by the body.

~

i give myself over to exhilaration   to the tango

*you are   this is
the beginning*

                              a stellarscape of dancers of stars emptying
itself of light emitting commingling with others

        a sad thought danced

                for what will take your breath
                                away you come to this dance hall

to this place of bodies   spirits waiting

                        for the one dance that will satisfy

                                your night you come

            to fill your vessel   to create
                        a moment of   wonder

                                ~

        if you are dancing the man's role, you must be confident,
        deliberate, precisely knowing what you want to do and
        what you ask your partner to do. you must hold her
        securely, as if this will be the last dance in which you are
        intimate with her. and most importantly, you must play
        with her, listen to her, watch her. what is she suggesting,
        what is she asking?

        if dancing the woman's role, you must interpret the
        leader's signals. you must quiet yourself and listen to
        what the leader is asking, hinting; and thus, flowing as
        a part of the other's body. if you are knowledgeable, at
        certain points in the dance, you may initiate as well. you
        may tease, your legs running up the length of his thighs.
        you can be in earnest, the gallant lady, the seductress.

y todo a media luz, . . . a media luz los besos,

all in half light
you stand you dance you exist   your being
bathed in the half light of the night   of each other

the woman's heels learn that they don't need to touch the
ground all the time. but the toe, the balls of the feet will
skim the ground as if it were shadow to its shadow. your
legs and feet will learn to articulate for you. your muscles
are relaxed, always relaxed. there is the essence of the sea
in your movements, the rhythms of mermaids, music of
waves and the busy-ness of the port. you tread as if on
slippery shells. slowly, your body will learn your partner's
movements, as if swimming with the tides.

you learn to respond to your partner's intentions,
interpreting your partner's signals.

to use in a way hands
place them in a way

a signature

complicated yet
elegant & nostalgic the music

violins cellos   *bandoneónes*
a piano   sometimes a trombone

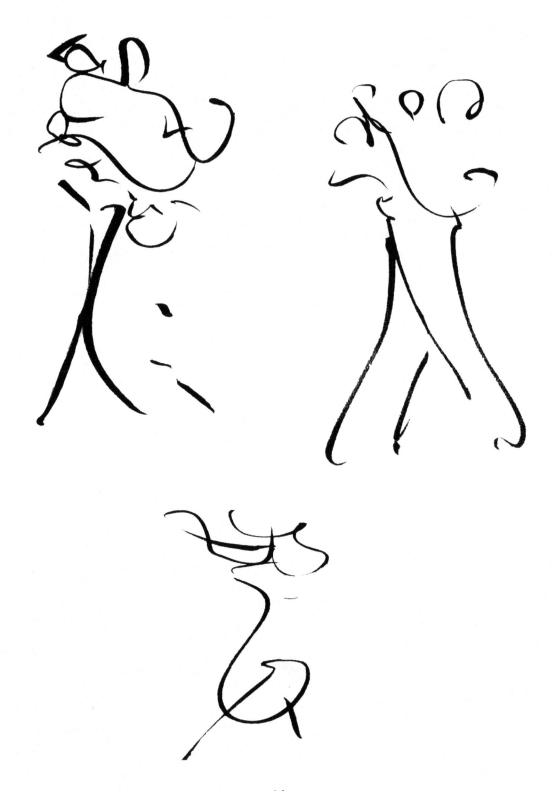

veins floors run   hearts beat together

embraces on the dance floor   hands intertwined

                    the brace of spirit   a ferris wheel

                            animating the floor

        what is the matter of love?   a leaf deftly decomposed
                    a monsoon of rain

                        an act? embroidered dancing

            branch carrying wind   cave blue

                                saintly neurons &
                                    possibility

        un pensamiento triste que se baila

joy is a musty bird a titan shore
                when thunder strikes
                                orange flares the milonga blue

        each cadence danced to magnified   tripled

2

      fearlessly the tango envelopes

[quizzical]

are you delusions' skin?

are you the *tanguero* or the tango?

the dancer or the dance

    are you shoes' beat?

are you woman's dress? are you the hazy hair of
the violin's bow?

are you the music itself ubiquitous   transforming?

the *bandoneón's* vibrato?

are you woman's heel?
       man's hell, or forehead leading?

       you are a slinking cat prowling
          fearlessly allowing the music
              to seep into your consciousness
         walking the tango walk

the tango is elliptical, circular & geometric. you are
perhaps inevitably working on a mathematical equation
as you are dancing. shapes enter your arena of influence:
triangles, squares, circles, never-ending spirals. you turn
around him; he turns about you. you move around him,
following the music's beat, the accordion's pulse, heart's
rhythms. you think of everything at once, ferris wheels,
rain, an autumn leaf drifting, the swell of morning dew,
flying.

      the dance, circular, carries you on the wind of its
music. evening blue, joy on a twilight shore.

19

there is a saying, or joke, about the differences between
the three types of tangos:

American tango is the beginning of a relationship: the
partners are cordial with one another, getting to know
each other.

Argentine tango is the high noon of a love affair: the
partners are passionate, discovering each other's mysteries.

International tango is the coldness after a broken marriage:
the partners must deal with each other, snapping heads
fiercely like eagles.

~

the next day it will grow
larger than life

more lucid more intangible more
mysterious
crepuscular ethereal

first the essence of balance

                                                 tendons outstretched

shells undersea

                                                 to use in a way feet
                                                       place them in a way

                                                       the foot a signature

                                               adroitly seductively

through you i exist

            of your thought
                        of your body and steps your dance

                  an extension of myself

                    content mingling with music

                                          Tango que fuiste feliz
                                          como yo también lo he sido . . . .

3

the leader must not only consider his moves & what he
will initiate, but must also consider what the follower is
suggesting by her gestures, what "she is saying." he must
consider how she turns around him, a planet around the
sun. when is it appropriate to do a *parada*, a stop? at
the moment of a *parada*, she has complete freedom to
do her adornments or initiate a move. this is one of the
few moments in the dance in which she has complete
freedom.

~

whorls leading to
eyes   pupils

through arms   elbows intact
by voice &   ear

the cochlea

a spiral leading to the sea

vibes of the piano keys—struck

through voice & esteem
whip   of daisies   sirens with ebullient hair

water a fluid   sensible & level-headed

24

am i describing you

        then?

             between us

                a hand leading to sublime
                    happenings

color exists through its absence

          love *is*

             amplified

                  let's underline

              space   divulge
                     these
                  moments

     details   the shore   shape of an embrace
                    shape of ether

      round bliss

the night making its trails in our entrails
    the music making its grooves
            worn into our ears

i have been happy dancing with you . . . .

       why are nails & tendons so dull?

   how is fire deadly?

       this tango beats a path
          to the heart

the follower's feet move as an extension of the other's
body. if you could put it into words you might begin to
realize you are doing something slightly sinful.
because you are imitating the passion of music, of heart,
you will feel yourself close to lust, close to luxury.

your muscles must be relaxed, at any moment, ready to
move, ready to react, a perched cat.

~

the world shuffles yet stands still

what has happened to me in my life   how did i get here?

how have i become such an addict of email? how have i slobbered over the messages

in habit of no time
i watch the love sift   dove away
watch the flash

of sun

paper flying   days
nights throttle the adorned space

winter gets so cold
earth's revolutions have affected people's sleeping   laundry

nor have i noticed the children skipping laughing
a woman scar-faced

watching the tangos come & go
the morning shedding its silvery skin

26

we dwell in the body of our knowing
                    year of dragon conversations   year of rooster
        revelations

nothing stays but eyes' marking   hands marking   birds opening sky

                        this dream this compilation this language of body moving
            through mind

                            matter balanced

    rats on atoms gorging on burnt corn ashes filtered from sky

                        ~

                                during winters   i fall
            into stillness
                                of
                                    your deceptions

        summers in Buenos Aires   i fall
    into motions
                    of
                    your subterfuge

                                        a peso burns   trash burns
                        trees slaughtered   an economy burning
                                movement   desire

the job of the follower is almost as difficult as that of
leader—the follower must be light on her feet, develop
flexibility around the waist, be able to dissociate the upper
and lower body, be quick in responding to the leader's
suggestions. the follower must understand signals,
suggestions, & must be intuitive. this job of listening is
difficult, oracular, in the mundane world as in the world
of dance; so you will find that for the most part, women
do a better job of following than men. the follower must
be gracious, and give and give away entirely into the air
and into the partner.

~

love does not lie   love is a noun

are we truthful to the love permeating us?

are we truthful to our souls?

subtracting *us*   what are we?

from previous lives dropped

existing in tangos

4

of one mind

a hand flourishes   a foot metered   cadenced   danced

not to feel the other   divided

what histories are kept sublunary
                    secrets exposed to those who linger

of the stellar race lungs of steel   linger for the abominable
                            knowledge racing across the hall

                    what is an embrace?
            an umbrella

traveling by body   i am of many minds

                                                   walking   gliding

               hand that leads hand which signals

of four minds   extolling air   fire   water   earth   & the fifth element
                                        & the sixth

                  of seven minds
                     i enter the land of living
                                  stroking tango's locks
                cool jubilous as snow

        [enter the land of widows]
                        intruder idolatrous clutching smooth & clear

             motions contingent on the solar plexus

                             on the hip bone

how is the dance spiritual? the revolutions mimic the
planetary revelations; communion with a higher force.
a trust one puts into the music into the other into the
other's soul. a trust a blessing one puts into the tango
unit. an entrancement through music, through body.
minds clear, empty, listening to the music. separate
entities, yet whole, dissolving into the higher force of the
music.

~

the forgetting must come

(hypnotized   images   recollections

                                              by voice   subterranean
          messages)

     beauty broken

i am speculating on how i should live   without things with less
                              i am reminded of the first manicure in the desert

     the momentum of tendrils furled far

                                   listening listen

step into the illogical entering

this embrace

      we can't escape destiny

     but always going towards

the gait of pursuance

       cherished locking

   of hands

on what levels do you converse

other than this poor language?

when walking forward or backwards, the leader should place his feet where the follower's was. this allows for continuity, equanimity, and balance. the leader leads & the follower follows, but also the follower is followed by the leader, a circular motion, a conversation. the leader must listen as well to the partner, listen to what she is suggesting. it is a dialogue to which the two agree.

would you like to dance? *meaning, do you agree to follow me?*

~

from this chasm
    red lights   chaos

your embrace
is time-
less

your space yawns
the years of
discarded
    sirens
3 a.m. milongas

the oscillatory
foolish
the insane

make their way
into tangos

she raises her right hand to dance when the man raises
his. their heads touch lightly at the forehead. she
caresses the floor with her foot, tracing circles, planetary
movements, celestial motions. her dress is provocative,
her heel 4 inches high. keeping her knees together tight,
she follows the man's signals, body and hands. moving
in time with the music, moving in time with her partner's
movements, she waits, senses, moves and anticipates. she
is always giving, like water over the earth.

to dance as if cutting a figure in the air, with a suit and tie,
the man stands straight, sucks in his stomach, head held
high. his moves are bold, legendary, quick, swift, slow,
tender, gentle. he is the ballast upon which the woman
leans. strong and balanced.

yet art is androgynous

       you answered & came
pretending to be ordinary
    taking on different roles

we're doing all we can to prevent
      disaster accept it

5

should we live our loves

in the world that exists between our fingers
                            behind our eyes inside our hair
                                            under scalp
            in air & ascension?

                    or ready
                        by surprise
            the days passed in dance halls the nights passed in milongas

                                    fearful of self

                    born of the port   tango music   the *bandoneón*
of slums   immigration & poverty
                                of Buenos Aires' good air

            crystal residue of lives   centuries' scent

should we wake up   to this addiction?

shall we embrace each other   hit the selfishness out of ourselves?

as an extension of the other's body, her heart & body moves. you vaguely begin to realize you are doing something slightly sinful, dancing the tango. because you heed music's passions you feel yourself close to lust, close to luxury. at any moment ready to move, ready to react, muscles relaxed.

invincible time

an element swimming through

tonight
    i went to Confitería Ideal   & danced
          & found you

                with another

~

(when little i wanted to give so much
             the rest is silence)

if one could flatter the black tune the white rune

married   divorced
        eleven years kept in mind waiting thinking of someone

a gesture relates to how much
        one knows about one's partner

and relates to how little one knows

this relationship between persons things that are naturally drawn
    by the foot   the leg
        by a way of being

a philosophy an insistence of being

a mathematical equation of sensual pleasures

in the milongas, both partners, while dancing, stand on
their own axis, though both slightly lean into the other,
thereby applying pressure, as if creating one axis.

another couple stands straight, axis to the night sky.
another couple dancing *nuevo tango*, lean out from each
other, using centrifugal force for some of its movements.

el tango es muy generoso.

the tango, often stated, is a comment on the metaphysical
nature of being. it is a statement on our isolation, our
loneliness, our willingness to come together in times of
need.

foot & hip seize their magical stances

do you love through the body   or   the heart?

                                                                spirit?

i understand that love is all colors at once

                                                & potential   dropped from sky

                                stillness is what we strive for   of heaven

        we move together   from previous lives

                                        the body's exhilaration is never
                                redundant

                                is happiness of body merely?

the woman seduces, that is part of the dance: her legs,
her arms, her posture, her elegance, her bravura, her
willingness to tease. she realizes the seduction is part of
the tango's beauty. the man also seduces, by his skills in
the tango, his confidence, his creativity, his playfulness,
his embrace. if he is able to show her another world
through the tango, a visit to another dimension, he has
achieved the highest.

the music also seduces, irresistibly.

~

Yo no sé
si tu voz es la flor de una pena

i don't know   resigning myself
          to your embrace
to the exhilaration of your touch
          i don't know if your voice is the flowering
in my heart
                    or my soul itself

conversation without words

                    the momentum assures

one is carried

                    tendrils reaching eyes closed

every step

                    logical & watery

we can't escape destiny

                    dignity of restraint

                    again entering grace

the dance's short 3 minute life

            ~

      in the violin's bow a cricket whispers

                  the reality branch

            breathing

          a singer's voice

                  in the *bandoneón's* keys

                        a man weeps

6

both leader & follower must listen to the music, for the
music contains the keys to unlocking the tango, the keys
to dancing it. without tango music, there is no dance.

~

color exists through its absence
        black exists to offset white

                                        sound exists only for the perceiver

    the tango takes place inside   two hearts
                                        amongst a multitude of hearts

        without anyone perceiving

        we do all we can to prevent disaster
                                assume the robes of laughter
    divinely flowing

being love takes reckless dreaming time

what is the figure that prefigures the tango? the *ocho*
an invisible sign of eternity

the embrace   the *giro* revolving planets

power in the event   figure that prefigures

song & heartbeat
fierceness
such that would hurl voices
into the wind

where do they get their power the women without manicure?

~

your body moves as an extension of the other's body.
the other's body moves as a response to yours. you are
the music, heart close to the ground, feet touching earth.
the music desires, dreams of a new way to dance, of a new
vocabulary.

one has such knowledge
        such words made up of gestures   series of automatic muscular memories
   that life
      of movement

                impulse lure deliberation step beyond NOW

no response except to what is known
        a musical symptom of membranes remembrance

                    il y a des choses inconnues

~

when dancing as a follower, you should not use your
mind, but rather your body and heart. if you use your
mind, your dancing will be slowed down, your response
time delayed. your muscles remember everything that
your body has ever learned and done, so let your muscles
do everything for you. you must give into the other, as
sand does to water.

the embrace of the tango is spiritual. because you are
communing, dancing, with another human being on a
basic level, often you don't know your partner's name.
this is the beginning of tango, beginning without name,
beginning at the source. one's name is little before the
shared sentiment of tango.

~

lunar chasm
                    a dance hall   you know well

                              the person with whom you dance

                              will
                                        the *bandoneón* weep
                    tonight in our tangos?

liberty, improvisation, and generosity are elements of the
tango. liberty to feel relaxed, to invent steps, to improvise to
the music. a generosity of spirit that allows energy to flow
easily between two people.

~

swirling spinning turning

after a shower

the world smells after day

the world whirls on its axis   all places at once

your essence planted in my hand

like shooting stars   have you seen such

clouds masking?

hair whistling palm's digressions

feet drawing shapes on the ground

have we arrived somewhere? have we sustained?

scent of almonds

read the waves

forced to hit ground from that state of floating

suspended

i would skate than walk   limp than imitate

wandering in an idyll

of course the hollow could break   but what can one do?

read the waves   of music
                          i forced myself to hit the ground

a perpetual whim   mistaken identity
                          in the skate of possibility

                                              seizure
                                    of heart
splice   clenched   why this fire? this fight?

                    the music wants grace freedom liberty

                        the music will tell you what to do in lanes of fire

                              ~

anchoring her to the earth, he is her support, her ballast.
he gives her time to do her adornments. the woman's
heel sometimes touches the ground. but the balls of the
feet & toe will trail the ground, shadow to its shadow.
your legs see & articulate for you. there is the essence of
the waves in your movements; you tread lightly though
firmly on the ground. your hands learn your partner's
movements. you are pure breath, b-r-e-a-t-h-i-n-g.

7

remember

how it is when we are apart

you caught my hand it was

a veil of rain the dance hall a gleam

with eyes closed   with my being

in tumult

~

following the rhythms of the music, the *bandoneón's* pulse,
heart's rhythms. of everything at once you think, the
tough streets of Buenos Aires, its people and shadows,
the inventors of the dance, *lunfardo* floating in songs,
milongueros you have known, people you have loved. and
then nothing but the beat, the heart beating.

you, the leader, must not take away her power. you must
give her power, give her time to do what adornments
she wants to or needs to do. (the follower conversely
must give the leader the freedom to do what the music
suggests; the follower must listen and wait patiently,
allowing for anything to occur.)

you are confident, deliberate, precisely knowing what you
want to do & what you ask your partner to do. your feet
are planted securely on the ground, her ballast. you hold
her securely, as if this will be your last dance. you play
with her, listen to her, watch her. what is she suggesting,
what is she asking? all of this suggests the breadth of her
tango knowledge.

these saunterings illumine you

                              the days are slow and long   nights slower
                                    i believe i am dreaming

                 of what is necessary

our connections fermenting like wine

            a stellarscape of dancers

a sad thought danced

                for what will take your breath
away you come

for the one dance that will satisfy
                your night you come
      to fill your void   create wonder

        on the dance floor
               rapture

MILONGA: A SEISMOLOGY

Qué ganas de llorar en esta tarde gris . . .
En su repiquetear la lluvia habla de ti.

"En Esta Tarde Gris"
José Maria Contursi, 1941

MILONGA: A SEISMOLOGY

1

How many women have you held to perfect
your movements?

How many circles have you drawn
with your prescient feet?

How many breasts have you pressed   held the moment
in a tiny chandelier?

Backs have you crushed with your palm peppers on stone?

Through this dance what are the geometrical
equations you have considered?

How many shielded eyes from your radiance?

How many have had to forget?

Isn't complicity best
most dangerous?

Death pulsed, then you
appeared

watch the lily procession   *during this interim*

                                                        leaves circling

what *is*
only through gesture

the mystical logic of tango

flicker   *voleo*   thigh

demands

the concentration of an eagle's feather

                                                        my wife is in fact
                                                        a dressmaker

                                                        i would not be able to
                                                        bear not
                                                        understanding
                                                        this animation
                                                        this dance

2

for this dream is long i would not have noticed

when god allowed speech

in your arms
the hours between a breath   step & hand clasp

          liquid beat

tangled bodies enter ready
into another

between us one inch an arm-length hundreds
of bodies away

earth
earthliness
once i held you would it be too late?

the source
of the unexpressed
            in this tango

                                                    with cause   instigation

compared   *tantra mantra tomorrow*
to what is in me
                    compared to
what is in us
        compared to war widows rifles standing

into afterthoughts the skill
with which they are prepared my head on
        a platter insistence of silver

a prayer
lying down   moving while
lying down   the greater earth
dreams our movements

                                        Buenos Aires
                                        departures
                                        arrivals the scented
                                        trail of a tango
                                        miles
                                        danced

3

who remembers your name
        as the floor
                        remembers it? invisible etchings
        lovingly drawn circular oval fanatical

sensuous time
danced
in a thimble
within the smells of dew
in a favorite shoe
that knows all
the milongas
within a heartbeat
plebian streets
insistent
mending
of moves
within your luscious
skin lavender
avian

today was giggly cold
          hands flying in
                    the air

     were you waiting
          for the cistern to burst?

                                                  who could save the world?

                                                  those who believe in
                                                  a new state
                                                  of
                                                  thought
                                                  wherein people
                                                  kindly address
                                                  each other
                                                  dancing

two words two bodies
flexible

a monster two
halves   jealousy is a red dress
three-pronged stick   a tarantula

coy is a name   a trance

4

Sweetheart,

"truth is a correct mental
relation to some energy,
law or condition"

jealousy is a claw
a relation to a situation

today you are a fountain
immersed in your own waters

someone screams
no one hears

someone mutters   no one
bothers

yes yes i say

someone screams   none

¡Loco! ¡Loco! ¡Loco!
Cuando anochezca en tu porteña soledad

End of the end

the music won't start again

until the next day

this wound from which
this wound

i walk miles

around myself

allegiance to moon
& night

shapes forming
invisibly transforming

5

unexpected the
howl

(how is this possible?
where do they get the habit?)

                                                  whore

left & right the men come to her
the eighteen-
year old boys   the old men

when air stirs
it stirs from
thought of you
when music gathers
to form melodies
it does so flowingly
              from you

when sickness enters
when all is there

          you a constant

                                                  knock

how does love function / how does anyone
function?   *one must be sufficient*
       how you complement   *the other*

how does the poet wake verse from air?

      (the deaf woman speaks
      in hoarse tones   she is beautiful)

after the others   you

          approximate the sun's shore   *the veil*
                                               salvation solace

the moon's shorelessness

what do the runes say?   *a step logical illogical*
                                               improvised

      never expect

                                               wish

another
>   filament   *live this moment*

last night? remember dark rooms
closed musky smells
of old dance halls
falling ceilings
>   broken marble

>   what apes

>   these times

the cell of your eyes
>   is consequence   *oven of your eyes*

the must of
a mandate   a mandrake in earth

6

again African throbs
unavoidable

the tango walk a slinky
cat prowling   smooth
as polished amber

ochos forward backwards
the deliverance of infinity

axis held   upright

oceanic

to say of myself
is to say the same of you

he puts his head
on the virgin
kneels & lays his head

myself you are in this event
        of looking

[spotlight]   *is there nothing*
                                                      but your body dreamt up?

the dancer pledges herself to gravity
            longing to be of air

dignified a dimension
rarely visited

                                                      are "we" is the question

                                                      i saw at the other
                                                      end of the building a shift
                                                      auras then infinite white

the walk a wolf's rapacious
                          metered

distant piercing the look

barely awake waiting   the air rippled
            around you   *reality opened*

in this grey afternoon   i wanted to die

not merely cry   in the pouring rain i
spoke of you
                 like a mad person   clawing at the air

we are part of

                      the transaction

sediment
of the earth & city
carried

how rudely dare
enters reality?

seductive hints:
          above the music spirits grow
          tree-like
             merges a hand touches
          a cheek   lips touch
          inner thighs
                   like octopus legs

through veins
throats
splashing skin

      how can anyone bear the touch
      of a beloved?

                                        expect nothing &
                                        the unexpected

the lonely who come
      for contact
            in the smoky dance halls
dressed up face thickly-made-up

the soul her own society
      perched on cliff a rock loose
able to fall @ the least insistence

      old passion like rocks wanting to fly

the handwriting the footprints
are illegible   quickness
         not showing all

                                                            arch for air

can one forestall it?

                    a hotel in which to hide?

                                                            lover

of divinity pure

many of you walk thus   heart anchored

how many when laughing do not show your souls?

     (someone screams   no one hears)

to find you under rocks   bootsoles
          rustling feet of nails

inside a cigarette
               a lotus

                                                    i would find you
                                                    locked in a mosquito's eye

8

(how many times have you felt thus?)

inklings among
                              fingertips?
soarings around the shoulder
              blade   a rose in the lung
a pitcher in the heart
                      vines in the veins

                                        goaded by the invisible

i am dreaming aloud
              can you hear?

                                        Winds blow!
                                                Let the avalanche begin!

sit & watch the dance floor
           arabesques
the lily procession
spinning logically   with restraint

of the cold atmospheric universe in space

                    handling the forces

                                        dollface
                                        you live one minute away by car?
                                        i would see you walking home i
                                        thought you must have taken the bus

must we live this timeline
of here & now
and not the future or the past?

let the dancehall go on fire from thought of you

when away

                                                                          a coffin-like air

drowsy anticipation of you
          under sea leagues have i slept

                                                                 my girlfriends wore flowery
dresses told me to go into
the milonga   i came in
cracked jokes twirled
around they thought i was
funny i took pictures of my
girlfriends in flowery dresses
it was wet & drippy even
inside but there was the
nervousness of y2k people
driving afraid of imminent
disaster we lived somewhere
else & mother wanted to go
out walk around to watch
the people drive badly
fearful
of themselves

9

i intuit you from air
        from intentions of music

from skin of words lyrics songs
                excesses   dominations

        racket of conversations   *undesirable*

in great amnesia
        to have a repertoire
                of moves

                in great dream   the undreamed
        is it possible to approximate
                        your dimensions?

how can anyone bear
the touch of a beloved?

        how can anyone bear the response?

subterranean world
                there are endless flowers
forehead to forehead dancing
        sweaty breaths
                a kiss between palms

                                        yesterday, in fear of killing
                                        instead of fighting
                                        i began to run . . .

through what cities have you roamed
      through which embarkments

          through what accidental thoroughfares
                         misbegotten streets
                                  shall i find you?

               @ what insane junctions in what
     corners undisclosed?

    in the avenues of silence
                      each eye
      undisturbed   inward

perfect energy transference

that was the power between us
                    intimacy without naming

these were perfect statements
declared through your chest
& body   this
                        i understand to be
            tango

they walk in &
out of each other's dreams
more like an elaborate
tango   improvised
each leading at turns
following at turns

11

in which dance halls
          will i find you?

                                                                    you are ubiquitous

in which songs will i find you
droning in
lunfardo

each strain of the violin each bandoneon's
          tilt

                              the floor you caress
                    dove-like

     flashing shoes skirt parted thigh

you are the champagne in those eager eyes
                              watching

          high heeled feet involved
                    in impersonations

watching others dance
i construct a story
      red lusty strains
          a story without you

     in the gap
neurotransmitter conspiring
a higher force the hand
the neurons its own life
constructing

a new tango vocabulary
not just
          giro   *voleo* *ochos*

     but one of the heart's
delineations

know what my hands say know its tones
               they are thinking

        sensations quiet   touched

shoe dares speak
        of you   its quiet lisping etiquette

incidental evenings reft of meaning
                  refer to you

while awake i dream
ridiculously sinuous
unrelenting
     dreams
        then to breathe
           you

                      she has spiders
                      up her skirt
                      a complicated woman
                      with complicated desires

it should come off light but doesn't
            should deter to wind
       but knows its own mind

branches clamor your name
               verdigris leaves

12

to see you in pitch darkness

stoked

the night was pale unheavenly

you are absent   this must be real
        for it is in the air

                a continuum

where do we begin   where do we end?

how does the soul fire its pain
        in these wilting summer days

a canoe finds the ocean
one leg finds the other
a foot taps
the other
& fall into
precision

legs & feet find their movements
        from the head
                        & heart

                how does the soul
                        forgive?

101

why is this route dangerous
        this unpaved route

keep your own counsel

my body doesn't
      know entirely what will come
from you
        that is the freedom
             of tango

what you think is felt
green & purple

what you imagine
      if long enough becomes reality

the man eternally
looks outward

she has left him again
for another

in the milongas   in tango we can't demand
        anything of each other
we must observe
            what comes forth

coincidence
someone throwing
a glance
an exclamation point
hand dusting a shoulder
turn of key
a hand a gesture on the back
            a swipe of
the leg
a brushing of breasts

        despite the blue heat

13

the pimps used
the tango to
test out the
women instead
of sleeping with
them they would
dance with them
first to test their
playfulness

blindly without memory without knowledge
                              of hunger
                    with laughter with insanity

you held my hand

              four months out of life
accelerated ways of thinking

your nails, it's a sinful color,

what is it?

"muddie potion."

remember the scent
          of orchids
                    orchestras
celebrated   in the background
                    the mustard heat sweat of moons

today is a gateway if you
want to step through you
should with a clear thought
in mind

what is the physical aspect of tango?

parted skirt high heeled shoes
geometry of the couple
dancing the angles created
by elbows knees
and heart   leader & follower

          the moon &
your perfume distilled through experience
                              & countless dances

pulses i drag my feet anchored
                    in cities engorged inflamed
          a feetless city

               through this dead town looking for you

the cards say change even
the i-ching. everything
points to falling towers
storms

106

14

my true one

. . . .

que ando muy solo y estoy muy triste
después que supe la cruel verdad

may the birds disperse & shower
    their wings upon the metropolis
   so people can gather the wings
    unto themselves

    their impulses my feet at no one's disposal
in a meadow real for we think it is   where
     we meet
   & not in this insane city or this scorpion-lit-corner

where every moment passes
    aware there are no corners
      no tables or driveways no
   mistakes or measles

  even in my unawareness
     there my love for you

   thick in moon & sun & wind

        wink

108

let me wear down the streets
                           forgetting you

cry out your name so my throat becomes
                  hoarse
                               no longer audible

let me reverse
            the actions of the wind

let me entitle you my organs
                          pipes full of wind

                  these sessions

let me undo death   to find you

                               nothing is real

15

will i go into the desert night a blind mooncalf?

will i relinquish   & forget you?

will i dot my i's forget that you don't?

one of the multitudes   lame

will i stare into the sluice gates & forget my own name?

how to gather the energy around me how to sleep

                how to civilize the winds?

                        how to continue dancing?

humor depends on someone
being there. it is dependent
on such a fact.
the same way it takes two
to tango

face to face with oneself
one knows what
      the soul is saying

      disjointed filmy
the freedom of forgetfulness
edges nondescript

of many minds
traveling in the land
of living
she stroked death's hair

the dancers are moving in a circle
in the dance hall
      each revolving around
the other

      it is love's function
            to explode
         in multitudinous directions

NOTES

On tango:

Most tango enthusiasts and historians say that the tango was born in the *Río de la Plata*, which encompasses both Buenos Aires, Argentina and Montevideo, Uruguay. Regardless of its birthplace, most people consider Buenos Aires to be the mecca of tango. Within the tango, there are three related but distinct types of dances: *milonga*, tango waltz and the tango itself. In the case of the *milonga*, it is not only the name of a distinct lively dance, generally considered to be the precursor of the tango, but is also the name of a tango social gathering in a dance hall, bar, or elsewhere.

Some tango terms used in this book:

Ocho: An "8" drawn on the floor with the toe and balls of the feet.
Giro: turning, with the follower taking the appropriate steps, pivoting around the leader.
Milonguero / milonguera: a person who frequents the milongas.
Tanguero / tanguera: a person who dances the tango
Voleo: a whiplike motion created by either leg and foot. The motion begins from the hip and extends to the toe.

~

My appreciation to the Italian publication, *Tango* (Collo, Paolo and Franco, Ernesto. Torino, Italy: Einaudi, 2004), for having in one volume the tango songs from which I used individual lines as noted below:

Page 1, Manzi, Homero. "Barrio de Tango," 1942: 144
Page 11, Ballesteros, Alberto J. "Dicen Que Dicen," 1930: 64
Page 15, Lenzi, Carlos César. "A Media Luz," 1925: 38
Page 21, Borges, Jorge Luis. "Alguien Le Dice Al Tango," 1965: 194
Page 44, Manzi, Homero. "Malena," 1942: 132
Page 61, Contursi, José Maria. "En Esta Tarde Gris," 1941: 124
Page 73, Ferrer, Horacio. "Balada Para Un Loco," 1969: 198
Page 108, Vacarezza, Alberto. "La Copa del Olvido," 1921: 20

ABOUT THE AUTHOR

A poet, writer, painter, photographer, and Argentine tango dancer/teacher, Mong-Lan left her native Vietnam on the last day of the evacuation of Saigon in 1975. Her first book, *Song of the Cicadas* was awarded the 2000 Juniper Prize and the 2002 Great Lakes Colleges Association's New Writers Awards for Poetry, and also was a finalist for the Poetry Society of America's Norma Farber Award. Her other books include *Why is the Edge Always Windy?*, *Tango, Tangoing: Poems & Art*, and *Love Poem to Tofu & Other Poems* (chapbook), the latter of which includes her pen & ink art as well.

Mong-Lan's poetry has been widely anthologized to include being in *Best American Poetry*; *The Pushcart Book of Poetry: Best Poems from 30 Years of the Pushcart Prize*; *Asian American Poetry: the Next Generation*; *Language for a New Century: Contemporary Poetry from the Middle East, Asia, and Beyond*; *Force Majeure* (Indonesia); *Black Dog, Black Night: Contemporary Vietnamese Poetry*; *Jungle Crows: a Tokyo Expatriate anthology*, and has appeared in leading American literary journals. Her paintings and photographs have been exhibited for one year in the Capitol House in Washington D.C., in galleries in the San Francisco Bay Area, the Museum of Fine Arts in Houston, for six months at the Dallas Museum of Art, and in public exhibitions in Buenos Aires, Bali, Bangkok, Seoul and Tokyo.

A Wallace E. Stegner Fellow in poetry for two years at Stanford University and a Fulbright Fellow in Vietnam, Mong-Lan took her Master of Fine Arts at the University of Arizona. She has taught at the University of Arizona, Stanford University, and the University of Maryland in Tokyo. She also has given scores of readings and academic presentations in Argentina, Germany, Indonesia, Japan, Korea, Malaysia, Switzerland, Thailand, the United States, and Vietnam. She has visited Argentina eight times to study Argentine tango and to dance the days and nights away. Visit her website: www.monglan.com